what is amazing

WESLEYAN POETRY

HEATHER CHRISTLE

what is amazing

WESLEYAN UNIVERSITY PRESS

MIDDLETOWN, CONNECTICUT

WESLEYAN UNIVERSITY PRESS

Middletown CT 06459

www.wesleyan.edu/wespress

© 2012 Heather Christle

Manufactured in the United States of America

Designed & typeset in Seria Sans by Eric M. Brooks

Wesleyan University Press is a member of the
Green Press Initiative. The paper used in this book
meets their minimum requirement for recycled
paper.

This project is supported
in part by an award from
the National Endowment
for the Arts

NATIONAL
ENDOWMENT
FOR THE ARTS
A great nation
deserves great art.

Library of Congress Cataloging-in-Publication Data

Christle, Heather, 1980–

What is amazing / Heather Christle.

    p. cm.

ISBN 978-0-8195-7277-6 (cloth: alk. paper)—

ISBN 978-0-8195-7278-3 (ebook)

I. Title.

PS3603.H755W43   2012

811'.6 — dc23   2011046139

5 4 3 2 1

for my parents

CONTENTS

...
iii

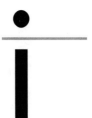

THE SEASIDE!

This is a wall of great intensity and furious
it kind of hums yellow and hums
green and never shall it hum purple Captain
when will you relieve me The wall
I love at night is huge and warms me
like a caterpillar or bag but do I also
have a family Captain or is the wall
the only shelter I have known and furious
why and humming brightly why Why
is all the beauty in the wall and not
in me Captain and in you Captain you
are studded lines of buttons That is
some finery! Whereas my outfit is it
like a prison with the dimmer switch
turned low No my outfit is nothing
the dimmer switch to nothing But
I can tell you things I'm not a piece of foam

SELF-PORTRAIT WITH FIRE

They asked me if I was on fire and I said No no no no
no no no I did not want to make trouble I was lying I was
on fire on my legs and on my hands I was ashamed I tried
to hide my legs by kneeling I set the grass on fire The colors
were a brilliant green and orange combination I liked it and smoke
I was not in pain or on pain I was on fire and lying why
to the people Obviously they loved me were warm and pink
and vocal on a promising spring day with electric buds Electrifying
I mean I mean bright bright bright like a likeness of me I wanted
to gnaw and to gnaw on an extra large slice of my likeness

TEAMWORK SHOULD COME FROM THE SOUL

They were projecting a hologram onto my snowsuit
A hologram of nature A snowsuit of white
Nature was not moving but I was moving and that
was most of the plot We got good ratings
They were going to release nature in Los Angeles
Houston and Maine but I was never going to be released
anywhere They were going to give me snacks and
send me into the tundra and evaluate how long
I survived It was our greatest collaboration
I thought Only they were the ones with ideas and
I contributed two things My body and the suggestion
that we should maybe try to write it down
When I died it would be a polar bear that got me
I predicted and tried to practice relaxing b/c
I wanted my last feeling to be relaxation
but they said that wouldn't fit in with the show

IF YOU GO INTO THE WOODS YOU WILL
FIND IT HAS A TECHNOLOGY

This tree has a small LED display
It is glowing and it can show you words
and it can show you pictures and it can melt
from one choice to another and you are looking at it
and it wants you to share the message
but it can't see that you are the only one around
and that everyone else is hibernating
which you love You are so happy and alone
with the red and yellow lights It's a nice day
to be in nature and to read up on the very bland ideas
this tree has about how to live This tree says
grow stronger and this tree says fireworks effect
This tree is the saddest prophet in history
but you don't tell it that You are trying to show it respect
which gets tiresome but then it flashes
a snake at you It's a kind of LED tree hybrid joke
and you could just kiss it for trying For failing
But it can't see you and it starts to cry

PEOPLE ARE A LIVING STRUCTURE
LIKE A CORAL REEF

People love to clean their ears and I love people
very much They are everywhere! Every single
thing I love I love for windows only and if
one window reflects another then friends
for me it's all over And in the windows are trees
and in the windows are people What are they even doing
with their hunger and in their new shirts They are
taking care of themselves and they are taking each other out
for lunch Oh even the rain has to love them People
are just too attractive! and the rain places itself
on the window in order to be closer to the people
the ones who are eating The ones who are
busting out vigor Oh people You have to love
people They are so much like ourselves

MOSS DOES NOT LOVE OTHER MOSS

It isn't dark yet though it should be dark
The grass is bright You can still see it
and warm and you can smell it and
elsewhere two people hold one another close
in a darkness they have created They can feel
their insides turning to olive oil and late late
afternoon light It's hard not to be them
to be like a fallen off piece of the mountain
to have traveled so far and still without darkness
to see the whole system The houses
pulling up from the soil and to want
the stars out now To want the stars out now
like a linen bag over the head

TO KEW BY TRAM

Lying down among the daffodils I am composed
but not the daffodils because I crushed them! Not
as an act in itself It was auxiliary Were my next
attempt to stand myself erect upon my feet
I would leave behind devastation
in the organized shape of my body
This is also how I move myself through
space Everywhere these holes I don't look
back to When I return as a giraffe the holes
will have to change They will say no god
would plan on such a shape And if then
I lie down again on these yellow flowers they
will teach me that my goldenness is dim

NO LIGHT AND NO HANDS

In the field there was a disembodied whistle
Disembodied by night which disembodies me too
I was in the field also I was in hearing distance
Hence I am telling you A whistle is often
just bad but this one I liked in part
for its dislocation It was in the field
with me but did not begin there whereas
I began there In the daytime I was a hole
but at night I could be nothing if I wanted
A wakeful part of nothing with an ear

AN ACTIVITY

There is a quilt and he is beneath it and some light
comes down through stitches He can see that it's man-made
Can see his knees and hands and belly and by the light
he knows the night lies in the future just as he lies
on the floor The quilt holding him together like skin
and warm and also with a soft all-natural light He thinks
from above probably he appears a rough organic form
Kind of casual like a canoe that's been attached
to boulders or casual like an island Like he is rising
from the floor and someone will maybe discover him soon
Give him a name and go away and tell a soul or two about it
How he was there and the quilt was there Empty young
and quiet like a prison yard when breaks the afternoon

HOW LIKE AN ISLAND

How like an island we are in love encouraging
moss & like an island we are barely moving Just
to exist takes much concentration & like an island
in love we have a house in our two imaginations &
they intersect It strengthens the house & our feelings
Unlike an island we wake up An island never sleeps
That is its duty & ours to remain in love barely moving
We do not want to disturb the house Do not want it
to fall into the ocean that is always so nearby It surrounds
us & is moving Like an island the ocean does not see us
or care why though we persist in loving it at one rate
or another & are waking close together in the dark

MORE OF FORM IS MORE OF CONTENT

As a child X is too small for the furniture The furniture
causes his legs to dangle over other junk such as the floor
and X feels woe X feels like dying or purchasing specially
made child furniture Small chair Small divan When X
grows to full size the feeling remains He is out
of whack with the world and it is like a crab
who walks out of its shell and that is not a metaphor
for X's emotional life His feelings are verified true
The trouble is when X is small X is very very very
very small and when normal X is very very very
very normal and in this extremity nothing will fit

TALK RADIO

There is only one thing in life that matters
It has to keep growing and it doesn't need me
Those are not clues Those are laws
The thing is the sky It is blinking I think also
I must be blinking as if to say Sky
you are not the only one outdoors with autonomy
and the sky stays very quiet
It keeps blinking like it is stupid
People think when something doesn't talk it is interesting
I am always talking and never interesting
like a pile of rocks Is that interesting
or moss wrapped up over the branch
but nature why don't you say something
It scares people when there's dead air

TAXONOMY OF THAT NOVEMBER

Then was an animal I could not identify and that also I lived with
In performing our daily headcount I noticed Then's skull
was shaped like a tiny cloud and yet I said nothing
I fed Then some hay and we were feeling wretched
in the blue pantry and at night we could not dream
There was a war on but still I got dressed
beneath the towering stars and no moon
According to the chore wheel I should have been sweeping
According to science we should have been dead
I knocked on Then's teeth and they were not hollow
like the sun was and I wrote it on my list
We enjoyed the taste of saltwater and baseball
we enjoyed on the radio in daylight
in a blue room that grew off the hallway
We were happy and wretched and cloudy
and setting fire to everything for warmth

WAY OUT IN THE COUNTRY

for & after Emily Toder

But how does it work I said Are there women
No women said the star I think it was talking
But if there are no women I said then who
were you surrounding No surrounding said the star
The star wasn't helping You should be trying
to help me I said and I wrapped my coat
around me tighter It was a cold morning
but the star wandered off It was hungry
and the grass needed trimming It was pointy
but if there are no women I thought who will help me
I said it out loud and the water was banding
together on the leaves they were unionizing Star
I said Star but it seemed to me now
there was no star It was painful I thought
I would be surrounded I thought I had thought

I'LL BE ME AND YOU BE GOETHE

I want it to be winter and I want to change
the color of this room This room should be
a blue room and it should be freezing
but ventilated and I in my medium snowsuit
irresistible I know because everything I do
I do to get more beautiful so you will want
to love me in the cold and indoor morning

MORE SWANS AND MORE WOMEN

A swan makes a bad pet It is a murderer
but very beautiful just like a woman
If you see a woman moving in the water
you must run away very fast to a mountain
It happened to me once and there
are no swans on a mountain
This made it lonely and natural so
I was very safe but I forgot
how to talk and when I came home
people could not see I was a woman
although I made a lot of statues to explain
and I live by myself in a cottage and
the water is no longer working It won't
make me beautiful just wet and the same

SUCH A LOVELY GARDEN

As captain of the flowers I tell the flowers Look alive
and they listen They have evolved like an ear I have evolved
like a piano Once upon a time I was not that dynamic Now
I am metric and a good listener a necessary trait in a leader
according to certificates I have had printed with very real
looking gold leaf with which I have a lot in common as
I am very real myself and with a nice patina and home

WALLPAPER EVERYWHERE EVEN THE CEILING

What is that thing that can happen A garden
is that thing You are walking around and sudden
Oh no dahlias You know that feeling like also
a family Oh no dahlias and you are giant with offspring
sudden all tethered in the world like zinnias dahlias
unabashed and blooming like another thing that can
happen love That is just an example Love is this
thing An example of love is the wind moves the warm
air square along a face and then love I love you tethered
like a rose sudden Oh no love and all alive in the garden

WE ARE NOT GETTING ANYWHERE

On the telephone there was a new message
It could have been anyone   It was the shark
The shark was calling to express his feelings
on his ugliness and his mortality
The two seemed related but the message was choppy
Where was he calling from
The shark said to call back   He was dying
He regretted that he would die soon
I did not want the message to happen
but it was too late I'd already heard it
There was a right action   How could I take it
Perhaps I could go rent a boat
He sounded sad on the phone with the dying
He was calling maybe from a boat

THE SMALL HUSBAND

If you want to talk to your husband
and your husband is very small
you lie down on the floor
and the floor is cold
but you warm it
and you look at the wall
where it meets the floor
You are five to eight inches
from the wall
and there are no other noises
Traffic everywhere has stopped
for the holiday
but the parade does not come by
for another couple of hours
and you are neither hungry
nor too full
and your body is a long silk bag
full of lightweight batteries
arranged on the floor
so it touches the floor
in the maximum number of places
and math has real-world value
it turns out
which is not all that surprising
and there are weekends and desires

gestating in your throat
pink and hairless
like mammals
and you close your eyes
and say things to your husband
but he is small
no make him even smaller

BASH

The woman is telling me what is
the most ordinary part of a room
and I agree with her yes it is corners
and I would like to move myself into one
but the woman has other ideas
or at any rate she does not have that one
and I open my ordinary mouth as if to speak
but find there is no voice there
and the woman has a voice that's like
California in the rain which is
another thing I will not say out loud
and I think also I love this woman
as if I were a cloud and she an airplane
that is to say though I do not speak it
that I love her in the ordinary way

SATURDAY

Journeying through our apartment I saw ants working
They just had no idea
You called them single-minded and I thought yes
I thought what does that look like in my brain
I was having a lightshow
Outside everything was falling off the trees
who like to draw
In that way and in others they are elephants
So enormous!   Halfway underground
The day was a crown we were all wearing
the trees and you   the single-minded ants
We worked and showered and rested by decree
We could see our domain   Our domain glowing
a lavender glow I did not mind

IT FEELS LIKE IT IS ON PURPOSE

You are everywhere in our home
The little stickers with your name
and our address   pictures of fruit
or birds   and just now
I was reading and stopped
and used your checkbook
to mark my place
It is the nature of things
to be used in some other way
When today I leave the house
I hope someone will see me
and use me as an example
of a person not thinking
about what is utmost
in his own mind
and without my knowing it
"the not-thinking person"
will be what I primarily am
and the world will go on lightly turning
with its millions of small adjustments
that make space for us
that let us get through

UP AGAIN WITH THE NIGHT

It's no good trying to talk to a roof
A roof already knows everything
It will only turn away
Better to stand on it
and yell facts at the stars
as if you were a real rocket
I'm tired of my constant apologies
All the sorrows I've whispered to leaves
who do nothing who tremble
who will not be appeased
I will be a leaf myself
resolved against sunlight
untouchable and hopeless on fire
in order to set fire to the sky
I am not sorry
I am not sorry
I brag to the planets
Who among you has the courage
to stay up with the dead
not to sit up afraid
but to lie down with them
And the speechless rocks go on spinning
and thus do I scorn them
and thus do I lay myself down
Lay myself ferocious
and in nothing's debt

THE ANGRY FAUN

I am so angry
I am a faun
I don't know why I am angry
Go home to your mother
I tell the bag
and the lamp shines
in a bright indignant way
Go home to your mother
I tell the lamp
Everyone has one
I bitch-slap the house
and my head falls apart
It's made of rain
This always happens
I am so angry
This African violet approaches me
It would like to calm me down
but it is standing in my puddle
It feels like I am being stabbed
Not repeatedly
Just one long stab
for several years
I wreck the violet
I trample all over it
with my two hooves
I collide with the mailbox

and we become one
This always happens
I am so angry
I am exhausted
This always happens
There is no reasoning with me
There go my reasons
You are a tyrant
I try to tell gravity
But my mouth is made of rain
like I'm a faun
This always happens
I am so angry
All around me angels
hum their wretched hum

IN ACCORDANCE

I come to you with knots in my hair
and the world in my mouth
I must kiss you
I come to you
Though the sun never visits me
and others break off my toes
because they are enlarging
Vladimir Mayakovsky—
Fine! I tell them
Fine! only don't undress me
I come to you and you undress me
with sand in my hair and tea in my belly
I love you whenever a truck crashes
into the low bridge downtown
and I come to you when trees
have the sense they've just landed
I am an excess—
my genes hardly need me
nor do I need anything
certainly not poetry
but bread maybe and tea
when I come to you
with my love in my chest
and my voice in my spine
When I am dead

I will come to you
having cast off these poems
which like me are an excess
Nothing makes sense to me
least of all movement
How is it you are in the next room
when I am so hungry
and I come to you
Is this the land and air
we spoke of with our two mouths
with our little spasms
I don't know anything
only your front side
when you are with me
and your back side
marching away
With my fists I object
to the stones
With my stones I object
to the feelings
In my sleep I will eat anything
and I come to you
with bark in my throat
and crime on my sleeve
and I come to you
full of my bones

THE SPIDER

The spider he is confused
b/c I am not killing him
only moving him outdoors
When I die I do not want
to feel confused
No I would rather feel clarity
like I am a pool
and death a chlorine tablet
I want it to feel
not like I am dying
but am being transferred
to the outside
And I hope I do not drown
as I have seen happen
to hundreds of spiders
b/c I love to swim
and to drown would
wreck swimming
for a long time
But death is like none of this
I know that death is a tower
standing in the middle of the town
And the tower receives
many visits
And there's no one
but spiders inside

DIFFICULTIES

I had a group of friends
who were anvils
They could not be recycled
I had been lying down for ten years
I needed time to think
I told the anvils
after they played a joke on me
Not cruel but not kind either
I was sensitive
I was a girl
Ten years later I was a woman
but more like an anvil
who could think and could love
in one direction at a time
and so had to be carefully positioned
because of all the effort
the opening and focusing of eyes
And what if I love the wrong thing
You can't take it back
It can't be recycled
Not like paper
Not like this dark glass

I AM COMING OVER

What you do is you have a what if
and then you go what is the consequence
so it is basically really easy
or also you can complain
like you can go this penis
doesn't make sense here
and then they have to move it
somewhere else
like go stand in the hallway
and move your penis around
in a slow uneven circle
that you are imagining
in your fresh mind
like you are inside it
and I am like I like that part
because I am also inside it
and you are showing me around
and in one hand I am holding
a glass of Dr. Pepper
and the other one is pointing
at what makes you different
and special and it is a physical thing
which I am going to touch it

A VERY REMARKABLE STORY

Always I am in danger
People might step on me
I might get moved around and then what
How will I ever get home
Other problems like plants bother me also
How am I to acquire one
Once it has been acquired
how will I stop it from mocking me
with its broad buxom leaves
It is shameful for a girl of my size
to be so cowed by horticulture
so I slap myself on the rump
and now every time I open my mouth
a daisy chain crawls out
What is the proper greeting for this
I'm shaking I'm all in a heap
But I still want to tell you a story
This one time I lived in the forest
It was magic I cried on my feet

AND THEN WE CLAP OURSELVES TOGETHER

This person walks off
to have a think
in the thinking place
The circle
It's not a manhole
You always think
it's a manhole
Sometimes our shadows are wrong
My shadow is of a staircase
but I am just a moat
I am looking at a man
and I am looking at his shadow
scratching madly all over
His shadow is of a king
He has been poisoned
and inside I can feel my blood
It is shining
Not in the name of love
In the name of cold glamour
And now the man has stopped
and keeps driving his truck
through the residential area
and I keep driving my car
on past the graveyard
The light is red
My appetite glistens
Oh sweet is the rain not arriving
and green is my overdrawn heart

WHAT IS AMAZING

1

That man thinks he is a man
but he is a candle.

Who will tell him?
He will be destroyed

and his wife will be on fire.
Life is tough for that man especially.

It is also tough for animals
who think they are lighting up

a lounge or ballroom
when in fact they are eating

and shitting like any other
chicken in the rain.

2

Take two rocks
and knock them together.

That will be the new candle.
Who said chivalry is easy?

The drawer where they keep
flashlights is empty

and the room is full
of quivering animals.

Safety is unreachable from here
but it is possible to reach one another.

3

If you laid out your wishes
from head to toe

you would be so far from home
you would need years just

to measure the distance.
Might as well start now

while it's still raining
and the governor's

meeting with friends.
Some animals

are friendlier than others
like roosters

who would destroy your face
if they could only remember

which one is you and which one
the source of all fire.

4

Do you know anything about
how to stop disaster?

If yes go home and save
what little you have.

All of this rain
and nowhere to keep it.

You need one dozen buckets
and an extra box of candles.

What is amazing is how
the animals won't stop sleeping.

It's like sleeping is where
they hide their goals.

One's goal in life sounds like
a match put out in water.

You might not know you've done it
but for the sudden lack of light.

WHAT WILL GROW HERE

another miracle is
to forget

in the garden to find
nothing with a name

to pass on through the green
as if it were an hour

gathered together by glass
as if to breathe

were to take apart the sky
and why not

if everything is moving
and down in your gut

there is that
borrowed blue

HAPPY AND GLORIOUS

The berries (which would sicken and kill you)
the bird consumes calmly this late morning

in its cold wet multiplying light
                        A light that shines

on only what could not be prevented
(Compared to absences occurrences are few)

One bird one cadmium belly
The whole blank diffusion of the sky

What I can say represents what I cannot

Grey snow filling in the driveway
Flown away bird to split the noon

PARKING LOT

Light breaks and its edges are sharp

O face wound bleeding profusely!
O pressure applied by the quick-thinking cloud!

If a man approach and beseech thee
speaking in voluble cursive:

                            What is the world and where am I?

tell him

        You are the ruined thing
        and the world is what loves to repair you

GO AND PLAY OUTSIDE

The declaration of light as read by shadows
and the leaf the wind lifts in an elegant betrayal

of the stillness the morning'd arranged—
what caterwauls, what loops the world

gives us, gives us *eagles*! And ugliness
it gives us too. What gives us away is not

the world, is its disappearance, how
still we breathe out as if we could hide.

SOME COMBINATIONS

Locked out of the cloud
my fright concentrates itself

within me like stars:
semi-permanent, bright.

A person is layers of instants
covered in dirty blue feathers.

I mean her consciousness is that
and in this warm darkness me too

and when people flock into each other
we achieve action and block out the sun.

What is it, anyway, to look?
It is to vanish some parts to a hum.

I WILL KNOW YOU BY YOUR RED CARNATION

The box probably full of live animals
or other animals has gone missing

and with it the sense of crushed sadness
to which we'd so lovingly tended

and now we have what on our hands—
not nothing but not the sky either

and time seems nearly correct
but that is its mischievous nature.

What is it that we are attached to—
stamps, ferns, nettles?

To have lost as we have so greatly
and to discover we still hold abundance—

how does this and anything happen?
We've seen the stars blown out

not returning and yet we have
also seen whole fleets in jars.

LADIES A BASKET

The feeling I had was becoming
to a person of my station

and the world from me pulled away
in order to reveal a spoon

it wanted to feature
There was light upon it

and my eye
            In my mouth
my infant tongue was sleeping

I gave my head a terrible shake
After that I do not know

what became of me
                 but of the world
became a wet and tasseled place

LAST TIME I WORE THIS SWEATER

That morning when weather erased the mountain
and I kept talking into the white like an American

and could see nothing I then rubbed the feeling
that all the data I had collected (the white) (the

mountain) (the talking) was draining away through
this vast and new hole with which I coincided

FOR HENRI

Blank road and then trees like a corridor
begin. How does that happen. How funny

for anything to start. It is the edges
we use to make art, but that is tough:

we live in the middle and so little in fact
seems to end. This dull continuous world!

Though a horse I think gets distinguished:
it runs, it knocks a loose blossom down.

TO DO

the noise of this machine
all day for company

all day so you won't forget
to end your body

where the skin ends
to fill in the pattern

where you're blind
to read the objects

as though they were a hymnal
and though untrained

to sing out the bridge
in the pattern and then

to hear what the world
sings back in kind

INFINITIVES

to wake to find the day quite flattened
to pull it over yourself like a lead apron

from under which you will not rise again
to finish at last the portrait of the cloud

and to look up and discover
now the subject has moved on

to grasp in hand a sadness
to know it's born of the evil

that rents your body's cold apartments
to see how completely your skin

encases you apart from god
the act of opening and transfer

and to weep at this out at the picnic
to weep at this onto your paper plate

ROUTE 109

I travel all day with a window before me
me a blushing bag
                        the world a pretty din

glass is the part I don't see
while all day apparent the sky

to which I'm no closer
                        from which I'm disbarred
the stony sky blank and unmoved

the air I breathe in was once Caesar's
to what do I owe this dim past

to the glass I'm a peasant
                        a fool
to the sky I am some kind of riddance

a driver behind a safe wheel
w/lakes to the side
                        a putative blue

CLASSIC HOOK SHAPE

Goodbye to the whacked-away clouds
& to what storm teams tracked
through the night
     There is no
such thing as replacing
except when on TV
they represent time
They ask can we zoom in
They say this event
and next door on some
other channel
     they're shooting
a gel in the shape of a human
in order to process
in order to see
      what holes
reveal in the body
Is that
   where the clouds go
What is this system
If there are thousands
of dark clouds inside me
is that
   what you'd call a disease

UNDER THE MOON THE KNOCKING

Was that a gunshot or
was it a look of temerity or
can you see the moon better
if you lie down on top of a rock

Oh soldiers your children are glowing
at such a great distance
they seem more like thoughts

DIRECTLY AT THE SUN

1

The window is dirty I learn
via dirty shadows on the floor

Thank you for the evidence
which I prefer and vastly

to the thing
                     the thing itself
And I know not what

I am the evidence of
though I am here

and leaning desperate
to prove it

2

For years I have been on duty
in this my body
    and this its mind

and no one has told me
when relief might arrive

but I think it will come
all at once by the hundreds

It will be a real parade
It will surround me

with great noise
    and with slowness
and coral and yellow and green

3

Do you know what time is like
It is like you are a pile of wool

and they tug and spin from you
until you are yarn
                    and this

is why we become upright
all the tugging
                    and why

too when we sleep we go
loose
            and I will tell you

another part darlings
                        and that is
your self is the sheep shorn apart

A LONG LIFE

It was like this.
We regarded the animals,
could not help but do so.
And light
which shapes wonderful colors
hurt our eyes.
They were too pale.
When two events
occurred at once
it made everyone laugh.
Happiness
I think we called it.
The air was full
of silver.
At night we kept out the cold.
A long life
lived slowly
in the company
of all our mistakes.
And how sometimes
in the evening
I'd cut what hair
you'd lately grown.

BASIC

This program is designed to move a white line
from one side of the screen to the other.

This program is not too hard, but it has
a sad ending and that makes people cry.

This program is designed to make people cry
and step away when they are finished.

In one variation the line moves diagonally
up and in another diagonally down.

This makes people cry differently,
diagonally. A whole room of people

crying in response to this program's
variations results in beautiful music.

This program is designed to make such
beautiful music that it feels like at last

they have allowed you to take the good canoe
into a lake of your own choosing

and above you the sky exposes one
or two real eagles, the water

warm or marked with stones,
however you like it, blue.

ALL THINGS BRIGHT AND BEAUTIFUL

Ideas come from the ocean
They walk out of there
They just can't wait!
A cruller comes from there
and also once some beauty
And when the idea
of people is over we will
walk right back in there
and make some jokes
toward commanding the waves
like we are long-dead kings
with a knack for rhetorical gesture
and that is how the ocean
will remember us I think

ACKNOWLEDGMENTS

Many thanks to the following journals, where some of these poems first appeared.

   The Awl, "Talk Radio"

   The Believer, "Teamwork Should Come from the Soul"

   BOMBlog, "What Is Amazing" and "Up Again with the Night"

   Broome Street Review, "Bash," "The Spider," and "Directly at the Sun, Part 3"

   Columbia Poetry Review, "Self-Portrait with Fire"

   Dark Sky Magazine, "No Light and No Hands" and "I'll Be Me and You
      Be Goethe"

   Everyday Genius, "I Will Know You by Your Red Carnation"

   Front Porch, "The Small Husband"

   Harpur Palate, "Wallpaper Everywhere Even the Ceiling"

   New Yorker, "Basic"

   Skein, "The Angry Faun" and "If You Go into the Woods You Will Find It
      Has a Technology"

   Slope, "I Am Coming Over"

   Tin House, "To Kew by Tram" and "All Things Bright and Beautiful"

"And Then We Clap Ourselves Together" was first published in video form on
The Continental Review website.

Many of the poems in part I first appeared in The Seaside!, a chapbook from
Minutes Books.

Lastly, enormous thanks to Christopher DeWeese, without whom this book
would surely not exist.

ABOUT THE AUTHOR

HEATHER CHRISTLE is the author
of The Difficult Farm (Octopus, 2009) and
The Trees The Trees (Octopus, 2011). She
has taught at Emory University and the
University of Massachusetts Amherst. A
native of Wolfeboro, New Hampshire, she
lives in Northampton, Massachusetts.